SUPER SIMPLE
EUROPEAN ART

FUN AND EASY ART FROM AROUND THE WORLD

ALEX KUSKOWSKI

Super Sandcastle

An Imprint of Abdo Publishing
www.abdopublishing.com

Consulting Editor, Diane Craig,
M.A./Reading Specialist

VISIT US AT WWW.ABDOPUBLISHING.COM

Published by Abdo Publishing, a division of ABDO, PO Box 398166, Minneapolis, Minnesota 55439. Copyright © 2015 by Abdo Consulting Group, Inc. International copyrights reserved in all countries. No part of this book may be reproduced in any form without written permission from the publisher. Super SandCastle™ is a trademark and logo of Abdo Publishing.

Printed in the United States of America, North Mankato, Minnesota
062014
092014

THIS BOOK CONTAINS RECYCLED MATERIALS

Editor: Liz Salzmann
Content Developer: Nancy Tuminelly
Cover and Interior Design and Production: Mighty Media, Inc.
Photo Credits: Jen Schoeller, Shutterstock

The following manufacturers/names appearing in this book are trademarks: Progresso®, Crayola®, Old London®, Gold Medal®, Mod Podge®, Tulip®, Sharpie®, 3M™ Scotch®, Gedney®, UL®, Roundy's®, Oster®

Library of Congress Cataloging-in-Publication Data

Kuskowski, Alex., author.
  Super simple European art : fun and easy art from around the world / Alex Kuskowski ; consulting editor, Diane Craig, M.A., reading specialist.
     pages cm. -- (Super simple cultural art)
  Audience: Ages 5-10.
  ISBN 978-1-62403-279-0
  1. Handicraft--Juvenile literature. 2. Europe--Civilization--Miscellanea--Juvenile literature. I. Craig, Diane, editor. II. Title. III. Series: Super simple cultural art.
  TT160.K87424 2015
  745.5094--dc23
                      2013043680

Super SandCastle™ books are created by a team of professional educators, reading specialists, and content developers around five essential components—phonemic awareness, phonics, vocabulary, text comprehension, and fluency—to assist young readers as they develop reading skills and strategies and increase their general knowledge. All books are written, reviewed, and leveled for guided reading, early reading intervention, and Accelerated Reader® programs for use in shared, guided, and independent reading and writing activities to support a balanced approach to literacy instruction.

TO ADULT HELPERS

Children can have a lot of fun learning about different cultures through arts and crafts. Be sure to supervise them as they work on the projects in this book. Let the kids do as much as possible on their own. But be ready to step in and help if necessary. Also, kids may be using glue, paint, markers, and clay. Make sure they protect their clothes and work surfaces.

KEY SYMBOLS

In this book you may see some **symbols**. Here are what they mean.

SHARP!
You will be working with a sharp object. Get help.

HOT!
You will be working with something hot. Get help.

TABLE OF CONTENTS

PISANKI

Pisanki are decorated eggs in Poland! People in Poland dye and draw on eggs to celebrate Easter.

COOL CULTURE

Get ready to go on a **cultural** art adventure! All around the world, people make art. They use art to show different **traditions** and ideas. Learning about different cultures with art can be a lot of fun.

Europe is a continent. It has many countries and cultures in it. Each culture has its own set of traditions.

Learn more about Europe! Try some of the art projects in this book. Get creative with culture using art.

Before you Start

Remember to treat other people and **cultures** with respect. Respect their art, **jewelry**, and clothes too. These things can have special meaning to people.

There are a few rules for doing art projects:

▶ **PERMISSION**

Make sure to get **permission** to do a project. You might want to use things you find around the house. Ask first!

▶ **SAFETY**

Get help from an adult when using something hot or sharp. Never use a stove or oven by yourself.

ART IN EUROPEAN CULTURE

People in Europe create many beautiful things. Some are for everyday use. Others are for special occasions. The **designs** in European art often have special meanings.

 **Tapas** are small snacks from Spain. Some people eat meals of many different tapas!

 **Alpine hats** are from areas near the Alps. They are worn in parts of Germany, Austria, Switzerland, and Italy.

 A **coat of arms** is like an ancient name tag. Knights wore coats of arms in battle.

 **Stained glass** is colored glass that is put together to make a picture or **design**.

 **Post boxes** are where people mail letters in England. Post boxes are painted red.

 **Quilling** is the art of making shapes with rolled paper. This art form is more than 500 years old.

 In the Middle Ages, European royalty wore **crowns** made of gold and **jewels**.

 **Wycinanki** is a paper craft in Poland. People make beautiful pictures out of cut paper.

WHAT YOU NEED

acrylic paint &
paintbrush

air-dry clay &
round container

bread crumbs &
flour

card stock &
tissue paper

colby cheese &
eggs

craft glue, Mod
Podge & foam
brush

fabric paint

feather

felt

glass candle holder
& LED candle

glitter glue

glue stick, hot glue
gun & glue sticks

ground beef &
ground pork

hole punch

jewels

measuring cups &
spoons

mixing bowls &
mixing spoon

newspaper

paper towels, plate & paper plate

parsley, garlic & onion

pencil, marker & ball-point pen

ribbon

rubber band

ruler

salsa & vegetable oil

saucepan, frying pan & tongs

scissors

sharp knife, cutting board & spoon

small rolls

tape & double-sided tape

toothpicks & fork

twist ties

vinegar

white paper & tag board

white pillowcase & 100% silk tie

wooden dowel

yarn

MEDIEVAL CROWN

Feel like royalty with your very own crown!

WHAT YOU NEED

tag board

pencil

ruler

scissors

hole punch

newspaper

craft glue

gold acrylic paint

paintbrush

jewels

glitter glue

yarn

DIRECTIONS

1. Draw a rectangle on tag board. Make it 5 inches (12.7 cm) by 12 inches (30.5 cm). Cut it out. Cut out a zigzag on one of the long sides. This makes the points of the crown. Cut out a strip of tag board. Make it 1.5 inches (3.8 cm) by 20 inches (51 cm). Punch a hole near each end.

2. Cover your work area with newspaper. Glue the strip to the crown. Line it up along the straight edge of the crown.

3. Turn the crown over. Paint it gold. Let the paint dry. Glue **jewels** to the crown. Decorate it with glitter glue.

4. Cut two pieces of yarn 12 inches (30.5 cm) long. Tie one to each hole. Use the yarn to tie the crown around your head.

STAINED GLASS CANDLE

Let the light in your room dance!

WHAT YOU NEED

colored tissue paper

glass candle holder

Mod Podge

foam brush

newspaper

black acrylic paint

paintbrush

LED candle

DIRECTIONS

1   Rip tissue paper into small squares.

2   Brush Mod Podge on a small area of the glass candle holder. Place a tissue paper square on the Mod Podge. Smooth out the tissue paper. Stick on more tissue paper squares. Overlap some of the squares. Continue until the glass candle holder is completely covered. Let the glue dry.

3   Cover your work area with newspaper. Paint along the edges of the tissue paper squares with black paint. Let the paint dry.

4   Cover the glass candle holder with another layer of Mod Podge. Let it dry. Put the LED candle inside.

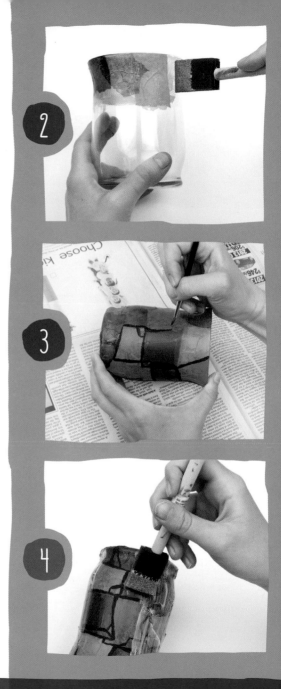

COAT OF ARMS

Make a medieval banner for yourself!

WHAT YOU NEED

felt

ruler

pencil

scissors

ribbon

hot glue gun and glue sticks

double-sided tape

fabric paint

glitter glue

wooden dowel

DIRECTIONS

1. Draw a rectangle on the felt. Make it 24 inches (61 cm) by 10 inches (25.5 cm). Draw a triangle at one end. Cut out the shape.

2. Cut three pieces of ribbon 4 inches (10 cm) long. Have an adult help you glue the ribbons to the end of the banner. Glue one end of each ribbon to the felt. Fold each ribbon and glue the ends together.

3. Cut pieces of ribbon as long as the sides of the banner. Put double-sided tape along the edges of the banner. Press the ribbons to the tape. Tape the ends of the ribbons to the back of the banner.

4. Use fabric paint to draw your favorite animal on the banner. Decorate the banner with glitter glue. Let it dry. Push the dowel through the ribbon **loops**.

HAPPY ALPINE HAT

Wear this cool cap!

WHAT YOU NEED

felt

ruler

scissors

hot glue gun and glue sticks

craft glue

ribbon

feather

DIRECTIONS

1. Cut two triangles out of felt. They should have two 12-inch (30.5 cm) sides and one 8-inch (20.3 cm) side. Cut out two rectangles. Make them 12 inches (30.5 cm) by 1½ inches (3.8 cm).

2. Lay the triangles on top of each other. Have an adult help you glue the short sides together. Then glue one of the long sides together. Let the glue dry. Turn the triangles inside out.

3. Glue a rectangle along the edge of the open side. Turn the hat over. Glue the other rectangle along the edge of the open side. Glue the ends of the rectangles together.

4. Use craft glue to glue the ribbon to the hat. Glue it above the rectangles. Stick the feather under the ribbon.

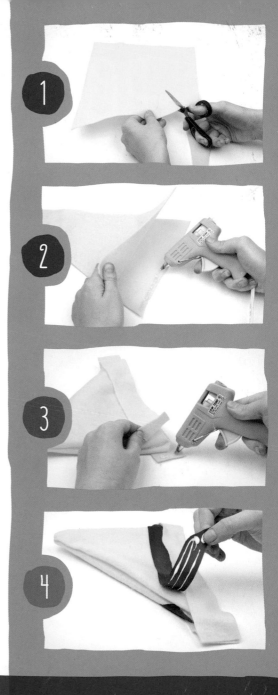

POLISH PAPER CARD

Create a cool card!

WHAT YOU NEED

blue, red, yellow, green, & white card stock

ball-point pen

ruler

scissors

craft glue

DIRECTIONS

1 Fold two sheets of blue and red card stock in half. Fold one sheet of yellow card stock in half.

(2) Draw half a tulip on one blue sheet. Draw it along the fold. Make it 6 inches (15 cm) tall. On the other blue sheet, draw two smaller tulip halves. Make them 3½ inches (9 cm) tall. Cut them out.

3 Draw three tulip halves on the red card stock. Make one 4½ inches (11.5 cm) tall. Make two tulips 3 inches (7.5 cm) tall. Cut them out.

(4) Draw three tulip halves on the yellow card stock. Make one 3 inches (7.5 cm) tall. Make two tulips 1½ inches (3.8 cm) tall. Cut them out.

(5) Glue the blue tulips to the white card stock. Glue the red and yellow tulips on top. Cut stems and leaves out of the green card stock. Glue them under the tulips.

PISANKI EGGS

Transfer cool patterns onto eggs!

WHAT YOU NEED

100% silk tie

scissors

eggs

twist ties

white pillowcase

ruler

rubber bands

saucepan

¼ cup vinegar

spoon

DIRECTIONS

1. Cut open the tie. Cut pieces of silk large enough to cover an egg. Cut rectangles 10 inches (25.5 cm) by 12 inches (30.5 cm) out of the pillowcase.

2. Wrap a piece of silk around each egg. The colored side should be on the inside. Smooth the silk close to the eggs. Hold the silk in place with twist ties.

3. Wrap a piece of pillow case around each egg over the silk. Hold them in place with rubber bands.

4. Fill the saucepan with water. Add the wrapped eggs and vinegar. Have an adult help you bring the water to a boil. Boil the eggs for 15 minutes.

5. Use a spoon to take the eggs out of the pan. Let them cool. Unwrap the eggs.

MAY DAY QUILLING

Celebrate the springtime any time by making flowers!

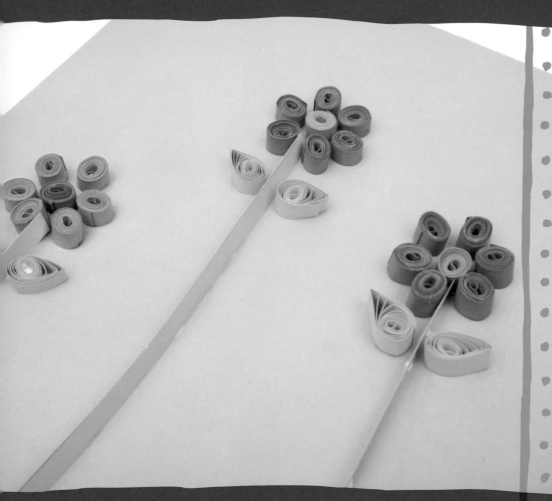

WHAT YOU NEED

pink, blue, & green card stock

scissors

ruler

tape

toothpicks

glue stick

craft glue

paper plate

DIRECTIONS

1. Cut a sheet of each color card stock into strips. Make them ¼ inch (.6 cm) wide.

2. Tape two toothpicks together. Wrap the tape around them tightly from one end to the middle.

3. Stick the end of a card stock strip between the toothpicks. Wind the card stock tightly around both toothpicks.

PROJECT CONTINUES ON THE NEXT PAGE

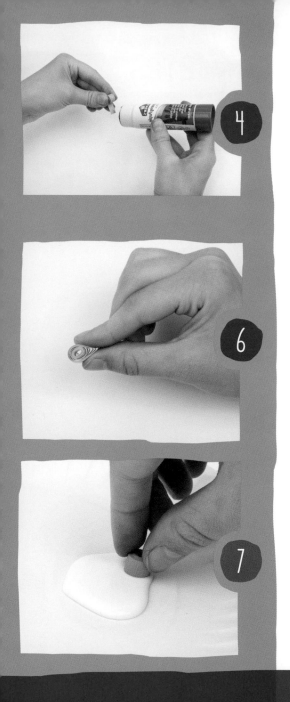

DIRECTIONS (CONTINUED)

(4) Slide the card stock off the toothpicks. Glue the end of the strip in place.

5 Repeat steps 3 and 4 with the rest of the strips. But leave a few green strips unrolled.

(6) Pinch one side of each of the green rolls.

(7) Put some glue on a paper plate. Dip one side of a pink roll in it. Place the pink roll on a sheet of card stock.

DIRECTIONS (CONTINUED)

(8) Add **petals**. Dip one side of some blue rolls in the glue. Place them around the pink roll.

9 Make a flower stem. Dip one long edge of an unrolled green strip in the glue. Place one end between two blue rolls.

(10) Add leaves. Dip one side of two green rolls in the glue. Put them on either side of the stem. Let the glue dry.

11 Repeat steps 7 through 10 to make more flowers. Try using a blue roll for the center and pink rolls for the petals.

POST BOX BANK

Save your money in an English post box!

LAURA'S
POST BOX
PICK UP AT
4:00PM

clean round container

air-dry clay

newspaper

acrylic paint

foam brush

ruler

marker

scissors

white paper

craft glue

DIRECTIONS

1. Use air-dry clay to make the top of the container rounded. Let the clay dry according to the directions on the package.

2. Cover your work area with newspaper. Paint the container white. Let the paint dry. Paint the container red. Let it dry. Paint another coat of red. Let it dry.

3. Measure 1½ inches (3.8 cm) from the bottom of the container. Draw a line around the container at that point. Paint the container black below the line. Let the paint dry.

4. Have an adult help you cut a coin slot in the container.

5. Make a sign out of white paper. Glue the sign under the slot. Let the glue dry.

TERRIFIC TAPAS

Make some delicious Spanish meatballs!

WHAT YOU NEED

mixing bowls

measuring cups & spoons

sharp knife

cutting board

mixing spoon

½ pound ground pork

½ pound ground beef

⅓ cup onion, chopped

1 garlic clove, chopped

2 tablespoons parsley

3 tablespoons bread crumbs

1 egg

½ cup flour

5 tablespoons vegetable oil

frying pan

tongs

plates

paper towel

1 cup salsa

fork

12 small rolls

4 ounces colby cheese, sliced

toothpicks

DIRECTIONS

① In a large bowl, mix pork, beef, onion, garlic, parsley, and bread crumbs. Stir in the egg. Put the flour in a separate bowl.

② Roll 2 tablespoons of the meat mixture into a ball.

③ Roll the ball in the flour. Keep making meatballs and rolling them in flour. Make meatballs until the meat mixture is gone.

PROJECT CONTINUES ON THE NEXT PAGE

DIRECTIONS (CONTINUED)

4   Put 2 tablespoons of oil in a frying pan. Have an adult help you heat the oil over **medium** heat for 2 minutes.

5   Put five meatballs in the pan. Cook them for 5 minutes. Use the tongs to turn the meatballs. Cook them for 5 more minutes.

6   Take the meatballs out of the pan. Set them on a plate covered with a paper towel. Let the meatballs cool.

7   Pat the meatballs dry with the paper towel.

DIRECTIONS (CONTINUED)

8 Keep cooking the meatballs a few at a time. Add more oil as necessary. Continue until they are all cooked.

9 Put the meatballs in a bowl. Add ½ cup salsa. Stir to coat the meatballs with salsa. Split the rolls in half.

10 Put a slice of cheese on a roll. Put a meatball on the cheese. Add a little salsa on top.

11 Stick a toothpick through the meatball.

12 Repeat steps 10 and 11 until all the meatballs are on rolls.

GLOSSARY

culture – the ideas, art, and other products of a particular group of people.

design – a decorative pattern or arrangement.

jewel – a precious stone such as an emerald or a diamond.

jewelry – pretty things, such as rings and necklaces, that you wear for decoration.

loop – a circle made by a rope, string, or wire.

medium – not the highest or the lowest.

permission – when a person in charge says it's okay to do something.

petal – one of the thin, colored parts of a flower.

symbol – an object or picture that stands for or represents something.

tradition – a belief or practice passed through a family or group of people.